ILLUSTRATED
AFFIRMATIONS

THOUGHTFUL AFFIRMATIONS
FOR A POSITIVE OUTLOOK

ANNETTE WOOD
THE VIEW FROM WITHIN

Have a positive view from within!

Affirmations are a wonderful way to help you feel good about yourself, and to increase motivation and self-esteem.

Using daily affirmations can lead to positive self-talk, and help you to motivate yourself and enrich your life.

Each affirmation in this book is a little work of art... I hope they brighten your day and uplift your spirit!

Create Greatness Every Day

Use this book in whatever way works for you, but here are some suggestions:

- Flip to a random page every day, once a week, or whenever you need a boost

- Keep this affirmation book in your purse so it's handy whenever you need a quick pick me up!

- Gift this book to a friend

- Use the affirmations as journaling prompts

- Share your book with a friend who needs support

20 Ways to Bring a More Positive Outlook to Your Life

While daily affirmations are a great way to think more positively, there are many more ways you can create a more positive outlook on life. Here are some ways to practice an optimistic and healthy view from within.

1. When talking, replace negative words with positive words and make it personal. Use "I" in your daily affirmations. Instead of saying "This is too hard," say "I can do this" or "I accept this challenge."

2. Journal your thoughts. Think about positive things that happened in your day and explore how they made you feel.

3. Counter each negative thought with multiple positive thoughts. When you catch yourself having negative thoughts, take a moment to think two or three positive thoughts.

4. Forgive yourself for missteps. It happens. The important thing is not to dwell on them and keep moving forward.

5. **Laugh outloud and often. There's always something to laugh about. Smiling and laughing releases "feel good" endorphins in your body.**

6. Go somewhere that brings you peace and happiness. This might be a nature walk, a quiet place like a museum, an area where you can listen to music, or a park where you can just sit and watch the world go by. If you can't physically go anywhere, you can always go to your "Happy Place."

7. Surround yourself with positive people instead of negative people that make you feel bad about yourself. Is there someone in your life that always makes you smile? Someone that always makes you feel good about yourself? Try spending more time with them!

8. Add inspiring visuals and colors to your home and work space.

9. Look at things from a different point of view. When you can see both sides, you can eliminate some of your negative feelings.

10. Practice gratitude... there's always something to be grateful for. When you're feeling thankful, you'll feel more positive.

11. Live in the moment. Sometimes it's okay to stop worrying about yesterday or what's coming. Do what you can do today to get one step closer to reaching your goals.

12. Indulge yourself occasionally. You are working hard to be a more positive person. You deserve to treat yourself.

13. Believe in yourself. The only thing keeping you from succeeding is your own negative thoughts. Stop getting in your own way.

14. Dance and sing. It doesn't matter if you have two left feet or can't carry a tune. Crank up the music and give it all you've got.

15. Get physically active to release more 'feel good' endorphins.

16. Ask yourself, does this really matter? Will it matter next week or next month? If not, let it go.

17. Relax. Sometimes you just need to step back, breathe deep and relax to get the good vibes flowing again.

18. Be kind to others. Compliment a stranger. Do something nice for coworker or friend. Call a family member you haven't talked to in a while.

19. Read something inspiring every day. Follow those who inspire you most and see what they do each day to make life the best it can be.

20. Have a positive personal mantra. No matter what it is, these will be the words you live by each day that remind you to be positive. Some examples of a great daily mantra are:

I deserve to be happy

Who I am is enough

I am in control

I believe in myself

I believe
in myself

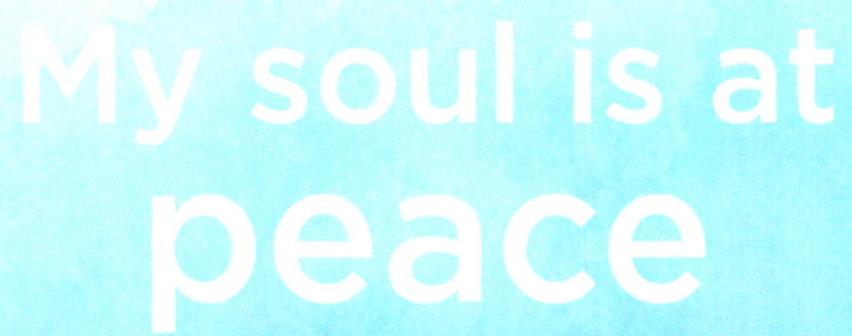
My soul is at
peace

I radiate
confidence

I am
grateful
for the
positive things
in my life

I stay
calm
when there
is chaos
around me

I am
optimistic
about the
future

I find **joy** and
pleasure
in the simple
things of life

I make a
conscious
choice to be
happy

I forgive myself for things I have done in the past

I am destined to find **prosperity** in everything I do

I am
bold and
courageous

I am worthy of happiness and love

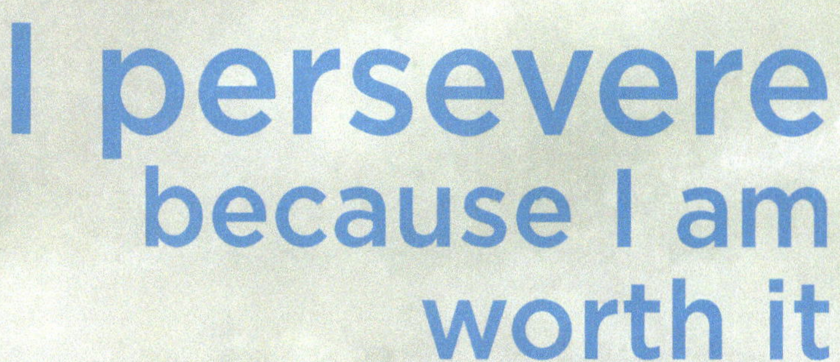

I persevere
because I am
worth it

I believe
in my ability
to find and
navigate the
path that's
right for me

It's my time
and I'm
ready for
the next step

The future
holds all kinds
of pleasant
surprises

FEAR

I free myself
from **fear**
and **stress**

I always
do my
best
because it
helps me
grow

I trust in my **ability** to create a fabulous **future**

I can choose
to be happy,
even if I'm not
in a perfect
situation

My **intuition**
and **wisdom**
guide me in
the right
direction

I let go
of my anger
so I can see
clearly

I love myself
and feel great
about myself